All About the
OLYMPICS

Nick Hunter

www.raintreepublishers.co.uk
Visit our website to find out
more information about
Raintree books.

To order:
☎ Phone 0845 6044371
▤ Fax +44 (0) 1865 312263
▣ Email myorders@raintreepublishers.co.uk

Customers from outside the UK please telephone +44 1865 312262

Raintree is an imprint of **Capstone Global Library Limited**,
a company incorporated in England and Wales having its
registered office at 7 Pilgrim Street, London, EC4V 6LB –
Registered company number: 6695582

Edited by Dan Nunn and Catherine Veitch
Designed by Richard Parker
Picture research by Hannah Taylor
Originated by Capstone Global Library
Printed in China by South China Printing Company Ltd

ISBN 978 1 406 22299 9
15 14 13 12 11
10 9 8 7 6 5 4 3

British Library Cataloguing in Publication Data
Hunter, Nick.
All About the Olympics.
796.4'8-dc22
A full catalogue record for this book is available from the
British Library.

Acknowledgements
We would like to thank the following for permission to
reproduce photographs: Corbis pp. 4 (epa/ Alessandro Della
Bella), 5 (epa/ Kay Nietfeld), 7 (Bettmann), 9 (epa/ John
Mabanglo), 10 (epa/ Kay Nietfeld), 11 (Stefan Matzke), 13
(epa/ Gero Breloer), 14 (epa/ Kay Nietfeld), 19 (epa/ Simela
Pantzartzi), 20 (Andrew Mills), 25 (epa/ Oliver Weiken), 26
(Reuters/ Stefano Rellandini); Getty Images pp. 8, 17 (Mark
Dadswell), 18 (Al Bello), 23 (AFP/ Michael Kappeller), 28
(Julian Finney); Press Association Images pp. 6 (AP Photo/
Thanassis Stavrakis), 12 (AP Photo/ Luca Bruno), 21
(LANDOV), 27 (ABACA); Rex Features p. 15, 16, 24 (Sipa
Press), 22 (Rex Features/ Warren King); 29 (Rex Features).

Cover photograph of the Beijing 2008 Torch Relay reproduced
with permission of Corbis (Xinhua Press/ Qi Heng).

Every effort has been made to contact copyright holders of
material reproduced in this book. Any omissions will be
rectified in subsequent printings if notice is given to the
publisher.

Contents

Some words are shown in bold, **like this**. You can find
out what they mean by looking in the glossary.

Welcome to the Olympics

The Olympic Games are a **festival** of sport. People from around the world meet to play and watch sport. The Olympics take place every four years. They begin with the **opening ceremony**.

The opening ceremony is a colourful party that starts the Olympics.

These athletes are running as fast as they can to win this race.

There are more than 10,000 **athletes** at the Olympics. The athletes try to be the best at their sport. The **motto** of the Olympic Games is "Faster, Higher, Stronger".

The first Olympics

The first Olympic Games began more than 2,500 years ago. **Athletes** from different parts of **ancient Greece** met at a place called Olympia. We can still see the **stadium** at Olympia where the first Olympics took place.

This is the entrance to the first Olympic stadium in Greece.

We can also see statues of ancient Greek athletes. This ancient Greek statue shows a man throwing a **discus**. Discus throwing is still a part of the Olympics now.

Statues help us to find out about what happened at the ancient Greek Olympics.

The modern Olympics

The first modern Olympic Games were held in 1896. There were no women **athletes** at the first modern Olympics. Now, nearly half of all the athletes are women.

Athletes met in Athens, Greece for the first modern Olympic Games.

Athletes from each country march together at the **opening ceremony**.

The Olympics are held in different cities around the world. In 2008, the games were in Beijing, China. Athletes came from 204 countries around the world.

Symbols of the Olympics

The Olympic Flame is a **symbol** of the Olympic Games. The flame is lit at the start of the Games. It stays lit until the Olympics have finished.

This is the Olympic Flame being lit at the Beijing Olympics in 2008.

The flag flies during the Olympic Games.

The Olympic **Flag** has five rings on it. The flag is a symbol of all the countries in the world. All countries come together for the Olympic Games.

Taking part

People who do best in their sport are given **medals**. The winners get gold medals. They are called Olympic **champions**. The people who come next win silver and bronze medals.

gold medal

Chinese athlete Zhang Yining takes the Olympic Oath at the Beijing 2008 Olympics.

One **athlete** takes the Olympic **Oath** at the start of every Olympic Games. He or she promises to follow the rules and play fairly. Fair play is very important to the Olympics.

Faster

Runners win by running faster than the other **athletes** in their race. The winner of the Olympic 100-metres race is called the fastest man or woman in the world.

Usain Bolt of Jamaica won the 100-metres race at the Beijing Olympics.

Cyclists crouch low over their bikes to go as fast as possible.

Cyclists have to pedal fast and steer their bikes carefully to win a gold **medal**. They have to be careful not to slide down the sloping track.

Divers jump into the pool from a high board. They try not to make a big splash when they land in the water. Judges decide who is the best diver.

Divers twist and turn over as they dive.

Pole vaulters can jump higher than a double-decker bus.

Some **athletes** see how high they can jump. A **pole vaulter** uses a pole to help him jump over a high bar. He must not make the bar fall down.

Stronger

Some **athletes** need to be the strongest to win a **medal**. Weightlifters lift bars with heavy blocks of metal on the ends. The one who can lift the most wins the gold medal.

Weightlifters lift weights that are heavier than they are.

Judo players wear loose trousers and jackets tied with belts.

In judo, one player tries to throw the other one on to the ground. The players need to be skilful and strong to beat their **opponents**.

Training for the Olympics

Every **athlete** at the Olympic Games must train very hard. Gymnasts train every day. Their movements must be smooth and **graceful** for them to win **medals**.

This gymnast has practised for many years to be at the Olympic Games.

Each rower pulls one oar to help move the boat through the water.

Rowers have to be strong and fit to row their boat through the water. They must work as a team to go faster than the other boats in the race.

Staging the Olympics

Lots of different buildings are built for the Olympic Games. A **stadium** is built for running, jumping, and throwing sports. The stadium is also used for the **opening ceremony** of the Olympics.

Olympic Stadium

This is the Olympic Park being built in London.

Athletes can make friends from different countries in the Olympic Village.

Athletes from around the world all need somewhere to live during the Olympic Games. An Olympic Village is built for the athletes to live in.

Paralympics

The Olympics are for everyone. The Paralympics take place just after the Olympic Games. **Athletes** with **disabilities** come to the Paralympics. Some of these athletes use wheelchairs.

These athletes are playing wheelchair basketball.

Eleanor Simmonds was only 13 years old when she won gold medals in 2008.

The Paralympics include many of the same sports as the Olympics. Eleanor Simmonds won two gold **medals** for swimming in 2008.

Winter Olympics

The Winter Olympics also take place every four years. **Athletes** compete in sports that need snow and ice. Skiers stand on long skis to slide down the side of a mountain.

Downhill skiers can go faster than a speeding car.

Canada's team won the gold medal for ice hockey in 2010.

The sports at the Winter Olympics are different from the summer Olympics. The winners still get **medals** for being the best. In 2010, the Winter Olympics took place in Vancouver, Canada.

Welcome to London

The London 2012 Olympic Games and Paralympic Games will be held in London, the capital of the United Kingdom. The Olympic **mascots** will welcome the world's **athletes** to London.

The mascots for the London 2012 Games are called Wenlock and Mandeville. Can you find out why?

Turn to page 30 for the answer.

80,000 people will be able to watch the 2012 Games in the London Olympic Stadium.

Many sports will take place at the new Olympic **Stadium** in London. People in the stadium and across the world will cheer the world's best athletes.

Olympic facts

▶ Michael Phelps of the United States has won more Olympic gold **medals** than anyone else. He has won 14 gold medals for swimming.

▶ The Olympic Games in 2016 will be held in Rio de Janeiro, Brazil. These will be the first Olympics in South America.

▶ In the ancient Olympic Games, there was a race for runners wearing armour.

Answers from page 28:

Wenlock is named after the village of Much Wenlock, in Shropshire. A **festival** of sport was held there before the modern Olympics began.

Mandeville is named after Stoke Mandeville, in Buckinghamshire. The first competition for **athletes** with **disabilities** began there in 1948.

Glossary

ancient Greece place where people lived more than 2,000 years ago, in the country we now call Greece

athlete anyone that takes part in a sport

champion someone who wins at a sport

disability something that stops someone doing things, such as not being able to see or walk

discus flat disc that is thrown. An athlete sees how far he can throw the discus.

festival party or celebration

flag piece of cloth that is flown from a pole. Each country has a flag with different colours.

graceful moving smoothly and skilfully

mascot person or thing that people have to bring them luck

medal piece of metal given to someone for winning something

motto words that sum up the aims of a group. The Olympic motto is "Faster, Higher, Stronger".

oath a promise

opening ceremony party that starts the Olympic Games

opponent person who you are trying to beat at sport

pole vaulter sportsperson who uses a pole to help lift him or her over a high bar

stadium place where lots of people go to watch sport

symbol something that stands for something else

Find out more

Books

Athletics, Rebecca Hunter
  (Franklin Watts, 2009)
British Olympians, Debbie Foy
  (Wayland, 2009)
The London Olympics 2012, Nick Hunter
  (Raintree, 2012)
The Story of the Olympics, Minna Lacey
  (Usborne, 2008)

Websites

www.london2012.com
This is the official website of the London Olympics.

To find out more on the Internet, ask an adult to help you search for "London 2012" or "Olympic Games". You can also search using the name of your favourite athlete or sport.

Index